This is not working

The center is not holding
We need to rethink our way forward

A reflective inquiry into our current condition

by
MIKE MORRISON

Copyright © 2012 Mike Morrison
All rights reserved.

ISBN: 1468119478
ISBN 13: 9781468119473

TABLE OF CONTENTS

Acknowledgements	vii
Introduction	xi
One: We Start From Here	1
Two: Which Path are You On?	11
Three: Spin	21
Four: Us vs. Them	29
Five: Small Voice Wins	35
Six: Is There a Dog?	43
Seven: I Hear You	51
Eight: Before You Can Change the World . . .	61
Nine: I Need a Moment	71
Ten: Moments of Delusion	81
Epilogue	87
A Final Reflection	91
About the Author	95

DEDICATION

*In loving memory of my mother, Marilou.
To Kerry, Zack, and Mackenzie —
my heart belongs to you.*

ACKNOWLEDGEMENTS

There are three leaders who have shaped my thinking about leadership the most during the last few years. While I have read and researched the topic of leadership extensively, it is these three who have influenced me deeply — and have actually given me hope that leadership is still possible.

Ara Ohanian, CEO, Certpoint: Ara has led Certpoint from a start-up company in 1996 to a global player today. Ara's genius is helping organizations translate their knowledge into differentiating results. He has worked with some of the world's most powerful brands, always bringing an "abundant sense of possibility" that is infectious. It is impossible for him not to lead.

Dave Harbuck, General Manager, Lexus: I may be biased because Dave is one of my best friends—but I truly believe he is an anomaly in the car business. The business is hopelessly transactional, but Dave brings a sense of purpose and people orientation that is transformational to all who encounter his presence. Like a great coach, he elevates everyone's game.

John Settineri, Director, Avery Dennison: I simply have not met a leader with John's passion, resilience, and learning orientation. John is one of the few people I would consider to be a true systems thinker, exhibiting a great gift to get up on the balcony. His capacity to create meaningful change is without limits.

Meaning is not something you stumble across, like the answer to a riddle or the prize in a treasure hunt. Meaning is something you build into your life.

You build it out of your own past, out of your affections and loyalties, out of the experience of humankind as it is passed on to you, out of our own talent and understanding, out of the things you believe in, out of the things and people you love, out of the values for which you are willing to sacrifice something.

The ingredients are there. You are the only one who can put them together into that pattern that will be your life. Let it be a life that has dignity and meaning for you. If it does, then the particular balance of success or failure is of less account.

John Gardner

INTRODUCTION

Neither comprehension nor learning can take place in an atmosphere of anxiety.

—Rose Kennedy

Welcome to the age of anxiety. The level of chaos and complexity in our external world is now matched with the same level of confusion in our work cultures. They are in total alignment—and that is not good.

This is not working
The center is not holding
We need to rethink our way forward

Our work cultures are losing their capacity to create enough gravitational pull to keep the organization "whole." The reasons are simple. First of all, there is too much stuff. Each year we unwittingly pile on new goals, strategies, initiatives and "other requirements" onto an organization already straining to meet its core missions. Who we are and what we stand for gets lost in an ever-expanding work agenda.

Secondly, we lose ourselves to the urgencies of the day, failing to protect time to build the kind of organizational capabilities and systems needed to compete in today's world. We also lose our desire and capacity to create meaningful change.

As a result, we live at the outer edges of our organizations, lacking connection to a unifying center. We will have to rethink our way forward — and it all starts with meeting our most core and foundational need:

Our need for meaning

Without question, "meaning" serves as the primary pathway for reaching our true potential as both individuals and organizations. When it is present, meaning cuts through the complexity of organizational life by bringing clarity and focus to what matters most.

At our core, we seek meaning to fill the voids of our individual lives — and leadership that can begin to fill this void will ultimately win our hearts. But let's be clear here: when I speak of leadership, I mean the act of **creating meaningful change** at all levels of an organization.

The need for meaningful change in the world is overwhelming. The good news is that each of us has the capacity to create positive change. **Creating meaningful change** is the pathway that seeks to develop the leadership voice in everyone. It is the only way we can fully respond to the complexity and rate of change that exist in the external world, and the personal challenges of making a difference. In fact, the most fundamental truth about leading is that true leadership comes from the person—not the position.

The reality is that those who lead primarily through position enable the large leadership void in our organizations and institutions. The differences between positional and personal leadership are significant:

- **Positional** leadership is characterized by control and the exercise of power.
- **Personal** leadership is characterized by character and the exercise of influence.

However, cultivating a personal leadership presence is not an easy path. Deep in our collective psyche are the traditional leadership images of authority, position, and status. There's a special satisfaction that comes from being in charge.

The most powerful path that allows us to neutralize and move beyond these limiting forces is the process of creating meaningful change. Change is inevitable. Meaningful change is not. When we are in the pursuit of meaning, everything changes.

Through the creation of meaning, we also learn to deal with the battle wounds inflicted by others in our pursuit of change. We learn to defuse the inevitable negative feelings that arise by cultivating a critical reflection and decision space that disables our automatic and ego-centered reactions. We learn to discern the most effective way to proceed — *with* and *for* others.

Finally, personal leadership development facilitates the distributed leadership approach that is most needed by our organizations and institutions today. The positional approach not only fails in responding to the core demands of leading. It also robs the organization of the broader accountability, participation, and commitment that comes when leadership is developed throughout the organization.

Poetry and Personal Leadership

Almost by accident, I have discovered the power of poetry in cultivating our personal leadership voice. Poetry doesn't bother to explain things in

INTRODUCTION

the literal sense. Rather, it creates an emotional picture and then pulls you into it wholly.

A couple of years ago, I was facilitating a leadership development session and experimented with reading a poem that I had written. It was a little bit of a risk, given the conservative nature of the executives in the workshop. But something amazing occurred.

As I read the poem, I could sense they were leaning in—not physically, but with a newfound presence. I could feel a shift in perspective, one that created a shared sense of vulnerability. For a few brief moments, we were a collective whole—and all that was wrong with us got lost in our new reality. The rest of the day became more personal in nature, as we became more accessible to each other—wanting to share more of our true selves.

I have thought a lot about how this special dynamic was created in our learning session. I believe the poem represented a personal and profound disclosure about myself—and the participants were only responding in kind. They could sense that I was seeking to communicate with them at a deeper level.

With a newfound excitement, I started to use poems in my leadership development sessions, and without fail they started to work their magic in ways that bullet-pointed PowerPoint presentations could not achieve. I also found myself writing more and more poetry—**systems poetry**.

I call it systems poetry because it is aimed at understanding how the world really works—and how we really work. People are systems too!

Weaved into the inquiry that follows will be ten chapters that represent the core themes that will be central to rebuilding our center in organizational life. Each chapter is accompanied by a poem and one or two reflection questions to get your viewpoint into the discussion. I have carefully designed this discovery process to help all of us to rethink and ultimately reframe how we will move forward.

Let's get started.

Poetry heals the wounds inflicted by reason.
Novalis

One

WE START FROM HERE

One of the symptoms of an approaching nervous breakdown is the belief that one's work is terribly important.

— Bertrand Russell

We live at the edges of our work cultures, returning home each day and asking:

How long can I keep this up?

Part of the challenge is that we rarely bring our "whole self" to work—the self that has the potential to purposely and passionately solve our biggest challenges. Typically, only the narrow self is invited in—the one that will fully play by the rules of the current "boss-controlled and culture-driven "game.

This is not working
The center is not holding
We need to rethink our way forward

We simply do not have the capacity to maintain separate identities and purposes for our work and personal lives. If we try, we will lose the integrity and wholeness needed to lead ourselves and others. The whole self brings a special vulnerability that makes it authentic. Our invented selves maintain a façade that unwittingly limits our capacity to live a meaningful life. We lose track of who we are and what we stand for.

When courage needs to be summoned, we falter. True courage can only come from the authentic self. Unfortunately, we are under great pressure to protect ourselves from the relentless external pressures to succeed by reducing the expectations for our lives, creating a safety from certain losses that will occur when we put our meanings on the line. Instead of growing, we shrink from our true selves.

More often than not, this leads to an unhealthy conformity — one that we cannot see. I remember a perfect example. I had announced my retirement from Toyota but still had a few months to transition to my second life. During that time, I became less and less involved in the decision-making but still came to the meetings. As a result, I developed an "onlooker's" perspective—not fully engaged in the fray.

From this objective perspective, I noticed two things in these meetings. First, much of the discussion was meaningless, lacking a sense of purpose. It was the non-productive side of Toyota's overly collaborative culture. There was simply too much passive agreement and a lack of real dialogue.

My second realization was that I led these discussions! In other words, I was more conforming to the current culture than I realized. There was too much playing along to get along and too much alignment with the dominant Toyota leadership identity.

Here's the deal: The whole self has enough self-insight and courage to know that we create most of our problems. The change has to start with us.

How to Read a Poem

*Here comes the first of ten poems.
Below are a few suggestions for how to read them.*

Always read a poem at least twice. The first time, read it straight through (without stopping to analyze it). This will give you a sense of its overall feel and message.

If possible, read it aloud. When we hear our voice, it connects us to the words in a special way.

The second time through, focus on the words — and look for their special meaning. Pay special attention to words that jump off the page, stir an emotion, or provoke a response.

Finally, always whisper the last few lines of a poem. This way, the soul can hear.

A STRANGE PRESENCE

I am here
All of me
Even the uninvited parts
The parts I used to leave
Waiting
In the car

Strange
It didn't used to be this way

But all of me
Wants to see
Hear from
Be with
All of you
The whole you

Imagine that
The whole me
Troubled me
Relating to the whole you
Difficult you

Crazy you

*But now we know
(After much pain)
It is the only way
I can
We can
Understand this mess we are in*

*We used to
Theorize
Analyze
Prioritize
And finally realized
This isn't working*

*Now we know
Only the whole person
Dealing with other whole persons
Can see
Engage in
The whole problem*

For the first time
We can feel
Really feel
How we
Really are
The problem

We start from here

Reflection Questions
"Achieving Wholeness"

To what degree do you need to bring more of your "whole" self to work?

What are the barriers that are holding you back?

Two

WHICH PATH ARE YOU ON?

My life is my message.

—Mahatma Gandhi

Our lives—and our leadership journeys—tend to follow one of two paths: the "conventional" and the "unconventional." The conventional path is driven by our work cultures—cultures that tend to thrive on action, activity, and results. That's why it's called work. So, when we are at work, we need to be doing something (anything).

Our lives are accelerating in terms of increasing complexity, unmanageable aspects of time, escalating expectations, and declining resources.

Welcome to the age of anxiety. In the process, we are losing our sense of community and our ability to be fully present for each other when we are needed most.

**This is not working
The center is not holding
We need to rethink our way forward**

Busyness gets noticed in work. It's praised by others. It also gives us a sense of self-importance (I must be important…look at how busy I am). Busyness also makes it difficult to relate to others who are not being swept forward with the same level of determination and flurry of activity.

Unfortunately, "busyness" also absolves us of our need to do the deeper and more profound work that will truly make a difference in our personal leadership domains. We can't stop, look, or listen. We are simply too busy going to meetings, saying yes to all requests, and "doing our best."

However, in the process we lose sight of the bigger issues that underlie our work. We continuously attack the surface issues, failing to identify and solve the core source of the problem.

Our bias for action is so strong that we no longer question, "Why are we even doing this?"

When we are forced to slow down, we miss the sense of urgency that comes from the "busyness" pace. In fact, slowing down (e.g., having to stay home with a sick family member) creates a sense of vulnerability that occurs when we get pulled from the game. We dutifully complete our responsibility to family but somehow it still feels like a distraction and we cannot wait to re-enter our go-go world.

Busyness, the wrong answer to the complexities and responsibilities of life, has never been associated with great work. To be in the moment—to be fully present and attentive to the person or task at hand—has become a lost art in our go-go, web-based culture. We are physically present but our mind, psychic energy, and deeper capacities have been unwittingly diverted or diffused by the three sins of distraction:

1. **Trying to do too much**: We often fall into the busyness trap, eventually becoming addicted to the high that comes from a caffeine-fueled over-engagement.
2. **Trying to do too many things at once**: We also fall prey to the multi-tasking madness that is enabled by our hand-held

and desktop devices that are grossly mismanaged at the personal level (leading to TADD—technology-assisted attention deficit disorders).

3. **Trying to fit one more thing in**: This is also known as the time management trap. We believe we can manage time, but it's the wrong focus and leads us to do dumb things:

   You look at your watch and it is five minutes before you meet a friend in the lobby for lunch. You could leave now and arrive comfortably in time—but you don't. You turn to your e-mail, quickly opening all new deliveries without fully responding to any of them. Unfortunately, the e-mail from your boss has a troubling tone to it, and the anxiety it produces follows you into your lunch date.

As leaders, we refuse to be swept along by this cultural current. We protect and enjoy slack time, savoring quiet moments of reflection and rejuvenation. We know that reflection is just as important as response. Through reflection, we facilitate our own potential to create meaning. We slow down. Go off line. We *think*—not just process information—and bring our fullest cognitive and emotional capability to the issue at hand.

You don't need a mountaintop. You just need to create some time and space.

Another key element of reflection is that we remain open to adjusting our ideas about ourselves and the world. By doing so, we learn to view our challenges differently. It allows us to counter the automatic thinking that generally leads us to the same insights and solutions.

Simply stated, the non-conventional leader is not busy. She has a presence that suggests the opposite—she has purpose. She also has the capacity to say:

Not Today

NOT TODAY

definitely not today
I am not in the mood
not in the mood for
honesty
healthy food
advice
housework
relationships
reality TV
reality
meeting expectations

today
I am off the grid
out of the system
1 in 365
a systems thinkers holiday
(hope) no one will notice
(disapprove of) my absence

too late now
already confirmed with a

*glass of wine at lunch
and a lustful yearning
for a one hour nap
(my only goal for the day)*

*today
is not about renewal
no, no, that would be too plan-ful
today is about recovery
recovery from the systems
that we work in
live in
be in*

*systems that deplete
and deplore our humanness
our humanity
in the name of
whatever*

*we can only change the system
from inside the system*

*and today I am off the grid
outside the system
on holiday*

I'll be back tomorrow

Reflection Questions
"Leading Life"

Do you lead life or does life lead you?

To what degree has "busyness" taken the place of a more meaningful daily agenda?

Three

SPIN

The truth is rarely pure and never simple.

— Oscar Wilde

We live in a world of spin and we are losing our sense of the true boundaries of truth.

Spin has gotten so pervasive and acceptable that the truth has become a vast gray area with expanding boundaries. We exaggerate, over-promise, shade things, embellish, slant, skew, show-the-best-side, promote, push, and position.

**This is not working
The center is not holding
We need to rethink our way forward**

We see the problem first and foremost in "marketing spin." Marketing spin is the process of creating illusions of value while keeping reality hidden. Everything good about the offering is highlighted, promoted, positioned, and exaggerated, while ignoring the "whole truth."

Unfortunately, spin will ultimately erode brand value. While the brand is supposed to raise the level of integrity between the product and the customer, marketing spin undermines that relationship by distorting reality. In other words, my experience with the product does not match up with its promise!

Our personal lives are no stranger to spin either. Whether it's the stories we tell or the presentations we make at work, the data is always skewed in some way. We position things. Leave other things out. We put our best foot forward continuously. Our report to the boss that makes current business conditions appear to be better than they truly are — that's spin!

The authentic leader sees the danger in spin.

Instinctively, he or she knows that when we spin, we put our personal integrity at risk. Our integrity is our center, our sense of wholeness, and represents our completeness as a person. When we spin, we end up on a slippery slope where truth becomes "negotiable." As the truth erodes, so does our self-respect. We start to lose faith in ourselves.

Integrity starts with being honest with ourselves.

When we are true to ourselves and others — even under difficult circumstances — our higher self becomes engaged in ways that we cannot imagine. We are infused with a sense of purpose that elevates our status. When we spin, the opposite happens. The smaller self emerges. We lose our feel and need for the truth. We end up playing the "smaller game" of rationalizations and half-truths, a game that soon becomes our life.

>**This is not working**
>**The center is not holding**
>**We need to rethink our way forward**

So, try this for a week. Be absolutely honest with yourself and others. Unflinchingly tell the truth. Be vigilant and on-guard for any deviation that might impact your overall integrity. After this weeklong test, assess the levels of anxiety, vulnerability, and overall well-being that you now feel (compared to previous levels). If you are like most, you will discover or re-discover this simple and profound reality:

The truth will set you free.

Pretty much all the honest truth telling in the world is done by children.

—Oliver Wendell Holmes. Jr.

MOSTLY TRUE

I have stopped listening.
I have heard this speech before.
I have also given it.
Many times.
Different words. Same outcome.

It is mostly true. But not true enough.
Not now.
Not after all this time.
You are (I am) hiding something.

I can tell by the language.
It is perfect – but not pure.
It is logical – but does not make complete sense.
Not after all this time.
No one really thinks (feels) that way.
Why do we talk this way?
Things are left out.
Things are put in.
I can tell by how you say things.

You are rehearsed – but lack conviction.

You are polished – but lack presence.
You know I know.
We have both been there before.
I see you (me).
I want you (me) to start again.
Listen. Listen.

I want you to tell me a story.
Tell me a story so true that it could be my story.
I am ready.
I am waiting.
Ready.
Waiting.

Tell me a true story.

Reflection Questions
"Achieving Wholeness"

To what degree are you unflinchingly bringing the truth to the conversation?

To what degree do others see you as credible?

To what degree do you see yourself as credible?

Four

US VS. THEM

We may have all come on different ships, but we're in the same boat now.

— Martin Luther King Jr.

The "us vs. them" mindset has become one of the dominant orientations that we experience in our work and personal lives.

Simply stated, we grow up in a win-lose world. We don't get a break from it. It's us vs. them.

This is not working
The center is not holding
We need to rethink our way forward

Who is us? Us can be defined at a range of levels.

It's our country, our political party, our religion, our favorite sports team, our school, our town, our club, our work group—any orientation that links to our identity, and therefore must be protected. We need to protect us from them—their country, their religion, their team, etc.

In many ways, we are drawn to the tension of us vs. them. There are a range of reasons, but deep down where we really live is this truth:

Our self-worth (us) is enhanced as a result of theirs (them) being diminished.

We see this most clearly in reality TV, which has become one of the dominant forms of entertainment programming. We love voting people off the island. So it is not surprising that we bring this "survivor" mentality to our work lives. Them can be anyone (our bosses, fellow colleagues—even our customers).

In continually defending ourselves from them, we lose our capacity to take the larger, abundant view. We don't see the interconnections, the common humanity that links us together. In many ways . . .

_I_ don't see _you._

I DON'T SEE YOU

That is because YOU are part of THEM
THEM are THEY
We don't like THEM
Shhhhh . . . THEY might hear you

I don't like working with THEM
Nobody does
THEY don't understand how WORK works
US understands
THEM doesn't

THEM are not us
In many ways THEM don't seem to get it
It is highly unlikely that THEM will ever get to be US
Not in this lifetime
THEM seem pre-ordained to being THEM
So sad, forever THEM
But THEM also makes me feel better about who I am

I am US
But mostly I am ME

US are ME's
I didn't make up the rules
That's how it works
US vs. THEM
ME vs. THEM

My friend is crazy
I tell her this
She doesn't understand the true nature of THEM
To THEM she says I see YOU
I see the good news in YOU
I want to do good things for YOU
I trust YOU
Even though I don't know YOU all that well
I see YOU
I want to see YOU again

Why does she say this to THEM?
My friend is crazy

Reflection Questions
"Us vs. Them"

To what degree do you promote (albeit without bad intention) the us vs. them mindset? To what degree are you seen as an integrator—an advocate for common ground?

Five

SMALL VOICE WINS

Few people are successful unless other people want them to be.

— Charlie Brown

The conventional images of leadership — I am above you, ahead of you, better than you — still dominate in our psyche. The non-conventional approach is probably best captured by game-changing insights of Robert K. Greenleaf, over a half-century ago.

In his book *Servant Leadership*, Greenleaf reveals a view of leadership that is grounded in a state of being, not doing. The essence of his work is that the most important decision a leader makes is the choice to serve. This choice is best understood as an expression of your being. It is more than what you do — it is who you are.

When we complain of the "lack of leadership" in our institutions, we are longing for those who fundamentally want to serve others. We have lost confidence in those who claim power due to technical competency or political savvy.

In the leader's quest to guide organizational change toward high performance and commitment, the insights and skills required **to serve** are not as clear and comfortable as the instincts for autonomous action. Managers at all levels are pressed to meet the competitive realities of the business day, which require setting direction, communicating clearly, and controlling business processes to ensure quality.

The challenges of managing in today's environment gives support to the dominant **"results-oriented"** attitude that seeks to bring order to the uncertainty and complexity of organizational life. Results-oriented instincts provide the decisiveness and ego involvement that make the world go 'round. But they are not sufficient to produce the kind of employee commitment that is sought in today's fragmented world.

This is not working
The center is not holding
We need to rethink our way forward

Something is missing. It's not the know-how or business acumen. The missing elements, the necessary condition for long-term competitiveness, are the **service** attitudes that managers and supervisors must integrate into the workplace as a key source of motivation, innovation, and unity.

This rationale is based on the reality that individuals hold a deep and driving need to find meaning for their existence. In fact, purpose, meaning, and commitment are difficult to separate in developing strategies to produce high commitment organizations.

The **service-oriented** leader recognizes the needs of others, looks for potential motives, seeks to satisfy higher-level needs, and engages the whole person. This type of leadership actively translates personal values into action. The result of this type of leadership is a relationship of mutual development that ultimately converts employees into committed stewards of the mission.

A service-orientation, however, requires the difficult cultivation of our "small" voice.

SMALL VOICE WINS

Big voice says
I am so proud of you
You know more
Do more
Have more
No wonder they don't get you
Don't like you

Small voice says
I am unsure . . . at risk
Is this all there is?
Can I keep this up?
Will they find me out?
I feel lost

I have lost my sense of wonder
I cannot remember the last time I was enchanted
with someone
Or some thing
Or surprised by joy

I feel vulnerable
I am vulnerable

(I feel alone when I am with those I know best)
This is not real
Not good
But where is my outrage?

My anger?
My guilt?
My deep, deep dissatisfaction with what I have become?

Big voice says
Don't be small
Don't play the smaller game
You know more
Do more
Have more
You are winning

Small voice says
No, no
I want my innocence back
I don't want to be big

I want to be small
Travel light
Go anywhere
Fit in small places
Be spontaneous
Open
Reborn in knowing less, doing less, having less
Being more
Big voice says
You don't make sense
This is not the path we have been on

Small voice says
I want to be fascinated
Lose myself in the moment
Be in awe
Tremble in the presence of the sacred
I want to be small again

Big voice says
(No response)

Small voice says
I am thankful for this life
All of it.

Reflection Questions

"Big voice vs. small voice"

To what degree have you cultivated the inner voice that seeks to serve?

We must be silent before we can listen. We must listen before we can learn. We must learn before we can prepare. We must prepare before we can serve. We must serve before we can lead.

—William Arthur Ward

Six

IS THERE A DOG?

In times of joy, we all wished we possessed a tail we could wag.

—W.H. Auden

I hope I don't offend too many with this one — but to get at the true needs of leading today, it is cat vs. dog.

Cats truly capture the conventional images of leadership: independent, self-sufficient, and agile. Not bad stuff. But at their extreme they start to morph into aloofness, incremental progress, and hidden agendas. Unfortunately, for most of us, this is how we experience our leaders. Over time, the demands of leadership take their toll, and our leaders gradually succumb to a detached, **cat-like** presence.

Dogs are totally opposite. The moniker of "man's best friend" in no way captures the true essence of dog, which is for me, the ethos of non-conventional leadership. They are "totally engaged and hopelessly transparent."

Dogs also love unconditionally and possess a belief system (proven by research) that is more abundant in its view than any other creature that walks the earth. More than anything, they believe you will come home for them. (That is why they are waiting by the door.)

My analogy continues:

- Dogs have friends. Cats have staff.

- Dogs are all in. Cats play their cards close to the vest.

- Dogs care. Cats don't.

- Dogs trust. Cats aren't taking any chances.

Dogs also bring an enthusiasm that is irresistible and always draws others in. As leaders, we can learn from dogs. We have entered an era where this kind of transparent, hopelessly abundant, and trusting nature can bring a sweet, sweet humanness back into an attention-deficit humanity. It centers us in the ultimate truth that we do not exist alone—we only exist for each other. Yes, there is a Dog.

IS THAT YOU?

Yep, yep, yep
It is you
Oh boy
Gosh, golly, wow
So, so glad to see you!

How long has it been?
Only 30 minutes?
Really?
Wow!
Seemed a lot longer!

Where have you been?
Oh it doesn't matter
I'm just glad you are back
Don't leave OK?
OK?
OK?

If you do
Take me OK?
Ok?
OK?

I just want to be with you
Who are you talking to?
It doesn't matter
I am listening
Mostly to hear my name
But I love to hear you talk
It reminds me that you are here
With me

Heh, wanna go outside?
Not now, OK
Maybe later
I'll be ready
How about now?
Oh, you mean later later
OK
Cool
No problem
We'll go later

Heh, you look sad
If you are sad I am sad

Are you sad?
It's OK to be sad
I will be sad with you
Maybe we should go outside
It's hard to be sad outside

Let's just be together
I'll be right here
Right next to you
With my eyes closed
It helps me to anticipate
What will happen next

I hope it involves me

Reflection Questions

"Is there a Dog?"

To what degree are you transparent, loyal, and hopelessly abundant?

To what degree do you believe in Dog?

Seven

I HEAR YOU

To listen fully means to pay close attention to what is being said beneath the words ... You listen not only for what someone knows, but for what he or she is.

—Peter Senge

With the urgencies of the day pressing at us, we often find that our communications with each other lack connection and meaning.

Here's the deal. All of us want to be heard—especially in our attention-deficit cultures where any kind of sustained focus is a premium. Unfortunately, our response is often to be more aggressive in getting our voice heard, leaving no space or separation between someone's comment and our "already formulated" response.

The traditional leader unwittingly compounds the problem. Feeling pressure to live up to his leadership status, he pushes to have his opinions heard, his points made, his arguments won. In a sense, he believes it is his job to advocate passionately. OK, to a certain degree, yes. But not all the time!

This is not working
The center is not holding
We need to rethink our way forward

So what now? Besides our ego-driven, amped-up, double-latte-fueled existence, we lack a "facilitative structure" for our informal communications. Here are some thoughts to help you reverse this troubling trend.

Whether you are having a conversation with one other person or are facilitating a meeting, practice the art of the "pause." In other words, don't rush to fill in the speaker's final thoughts and then rush to present your idea. Give her the full opportunity to be heard—and actually hear her. It is a little counterintuitive because it seems like we are giving up our fair share of airtime by not strategically inserting ourselves into the conversation.

Give her a few extra seconds after finishing her thought. This gives the communicator that brief extra reflection time to not only discover what she wants to say but to be fully heard.

This is the critical point. Once we feel heard, we can open ourselves up to hearing others. The "psychology of abundance" takes over. When there is plenty of food for a group, people will self-monitor and actually eat less. When it is perceived that there is not enough food, people will hoard, and actually eat more than they normally would. We do the same with our appetites for listening and being heard.

The "pause" also does a couple of other things. It shows respect for the speaker. It underscores the message, "What you say is important; is there anything else you want to add?" It also cuts down on communication time. When there is an ethic at work that allows people to complete their thoughts, they will do the same for others, eliminating the need to repeat messages or over-communicate to be fully heard.

The bottom line is simple: If you want to get your point across, make understanding the goal. When you try to understand the point of view of others, you create an opening for them to do the same. Amazingly, people will worry less about outcomes when they feel they are fully heard — thereby becoming more open-minded in their view.

Listening is a magnetic and strange thing, a creative force. The friends who listen to us are the ones we move toward. When we are listened to, it creates us, makes us unfold and expand.

—Karl A. Menninger

I HEAR YOU

For the first time
In a long time
I heard you today

I not only heard the words
(I always hear your words)
I not only understood the message
(I almost always hear your message)
Today I heard your story

Behind the words
Beyond the message
Is your story

It is a great story
I love your story
It could be my story
(In many ways it is my story)
But I lost track
Stopped listening
Became numb
To you

No, no, not to you personally
No, no, never
But all the stuff
That became distractions
That became the busyness in my life
Kept me from hearing you
Hearing your story

I think I stopped hearing your story
When I lost connection to mine
When I lost track of all the everyday moments that
When linked together
Tell a bigger story
Create a life

I keep re-learning this one thing
It is these everyday moments
When fully experienced
When appreciated
When reflected on
When shared

When remembered

Remind me of who I am

I heard you today
I heard your story

Reflection Questions
"Listening"

To what degree do you make others feel heard?

Many attempts to communicate are nullified by saying too much.

—Robert K. Greenleaf

Eight

BEFORE YOU CAN CHANGE THE WORLD ...

I'm nowhere as tough as my father. I really think that I am more open to change than he was.

— A. J. Foyt

We are learning to cultivate our capacities to fully experience the hope, anxiety, grace, grief, joy, outrage, humanity, and humility of the unconventional leadership path.

Before you can change the world, you need to understand it.

Conventional leaders seek to change the world through the force of their personalities, the brilliance of their strategies, and the resources that they can bring to bear. Unfortunately, their best efforts end up woefully short of the mark.

The core reason is that they fail to "see and feel" the systemic nature of their quest. They don't really know how "their world" really works, and "their world" will resist in a complete way any efforts to change it.

This is not working
The center is not holding
We need to rethink our way forward

Non-conventional leaders know a different experience in their journey to create meaningful change. At first they stand outside their system (their world, their organization, their community, etc.) and learn to understand it in an objective way.

From the balcony, they can observe with new eyes and see the "whole" at work. They see the processes that make up the whole. They also see how the system is in perfect alignment with its current outcomes.

With this new perspective, they can now dive deep into the system as a full participant. They become an active change agent, fully committed to helping the system grow. It is at this level they develop a true "feel" for the system — understanding its true nature and potential. They learn that systems are human systems, with the "humanness" adding a level of complexity and messiness that is not easily managed.

They see their special relationship to the system—feeling responsible for it—wanting to make a difference within it.

Bigger patterns emerge and the leaders begin to connect their "balcony view" (the larger, dispassionate view of the system) to their "basement experience" (the gritty, human, and up-close-and-personal encounters). Their rational intelligence joins with their emotional intelligence to create a special view that knows what is missing and what needs to be done. Moving back and forth between the balcony and the basement, they develop a deep sense of what's possible.

My friend Anne recently lived out this "basement to balcony" experience in her new job. She found herself overwhelmed during work hours — trying to figure out her new role; dealing with a challenging and non-supportive boss; and navigating a bunch of new relationships. During the long drive home (she was actually thankful for her hour-long commute), she would begin to untangle these issues into meaningful chunks. Once home, her spouse became a sounding board for further sense-making that would allow her to re-enter the next day with a sense of wholeness. But for two weeks, Anne felt like she was in survival mode.

It took some time but Anne was able to develop a healthy perspective and a growing understanding of her work culture (with culture best defined as a complex social system made up of very diverse and unpredictable inputs--people!). Within a few months on the job, she began to promote positive changes in her fragmented work environment. Co-workers started to gravitate toward her as a trusted colleague and mentor—further empowering Anne to create meaningful change.

If we are successful in managing this "basement to balcony" process, something very special happens. We no longer see ourselves separate from the systems we work in. We feel empowered with a special sense of efficacy that comes from a capacity to "see and feel" the systemic nature of our work. For some, the journey can provide one of the most satisfying revelations:

BEFORE YOU CAN CHANGE THE WORLD ...

I am the system.

But that's the challenge — to change the system more than it changes you.

— Michael Pollan

I AM THE COFFEE GIRL

It was just a job
A transition job
Waiting for a better job
I learned to hate that job

Taking coffee orders at the counter
Answering dumb questions
(Made me numb)
No one really saw me
Appreciated me

Nothing worked like it was supposed to
No one worked like they were supposed to
Made the boss anxious
Made me anxious
Unfulfilled
Bored
Like everyone else who worked there
We were without hope
We were lost in the system

Amazingly
Our shared vulnerability

Became our shared purpose
Became our reason for showing up
We started to see each other
Began to listen to each other
Started to see the good news in each other
We were in it together

Started to experience these fleeting
But extraordinary moments
Moments of synchronicity
Between us
Our work
And our customers

I got lost in these moments
Got absorbed into the flow
Lost track of time
(Stopped checking the time)
Became less self-aware
More aware of others
The system was working
(I was "working" the system)

Developed a unique feel for my role as the order person
Setting the pace for the team
Setting a tone for the customers
I was in the middle of the system
(and I liked it)

Discovered how small things matter to the system
Because everything is connected
To everything else
In a system

Small improvements amplify our work
Energize us
Draw us in
We feel responsible for the system
It is a system that serves
Serving others abundantly

I can see the system
See how it works
I can feel the system

It is a part of me

I am the system

Reflection Questions

"I am the system"

To what degree are you changing the system more than it changes you?

To what degree have you become the change you seek in the world?

Nine

I NEED A MOMENT

As happens sometimes, a moment settled and hovered and remained for much more than a moment. And sound stopped and movement stopped for much, much more than a moment.

—John Steinbeck

Creating meaningful change cuts through the complexity of life by emphasizing choice, possibility, and values—three key virtues that always enhance the quality of human experience.

The capacity to create meaningful change is sustained by our ability to be in the moment. It is in this safe harbor that huge amounts of sense-making, truth-telling, reflection and renewal can be exercised daily so that we can weather the storms that characterize any transition from the known to the unknown.

No matter how much we dislike our current place, the unknown future cannot compete with the comfort of a world that has hard edges.

This is not working
The center is not holding
We need to rethink our way forward

We also know that creating meaningful change has no chance of occurring until a commitment has been made. It is often the most important moment in the journey. Mountaineer W. H. Murray said it best:

The moment one definitely commits oneself, then Providence moves too. All sorts of things occur to help that would never otherwise have occurred. A stream of events issues from the decision, raising unforeseen incidents and meetings and material assistance, which no man could have dreamt would have come his way.

W. H. Murray

Unfortunately, we have learned to become artful dodgers at living out our true intentions. We allow life to incrementally emerge, one painful, cautious step at a time. Every day, we lose access to 20,000 waking moments that represent more than enough time to shape the change we seek in the world. (A moment is three seconds—an actual unit of time.)

It is our willingness to manage these moments that ultimately rewards us with a sense of clarity and focus that cannot be restrained. This sense of purpose draws others toward us. As Murray notes in the quote above:

All sorts of things occur to help that would never otherwise have occurred.

Over time, I have cultivated a range of strategies that have helped me to more fully manage the moments of each day. For example, I always take a few moments every morning to get centered around my need-to-do and want-to-do lists (see Epilogue for a fuller explanation).

Instead of feeling overburdened by activities and the rush of the day, I get to begin the day with a sense of empowerment that comes from prioritizing the things that matter most. The habit of morning moments has become a powerful routine that I simply cannot start the day without. (On those days that I don't make time, I feel untethered, disconnected from a sense of purpose.)

Here's what I know best: We have plenty of time in this life. We really do.

PLENTY OF TIME

I need a moment
Just one moment
Of your time

A moment in time
A true unit of time
Three seconds in duration

One thousand one
One thousand two
One thousand three

That's one moment

One thousand one
One thousand two
One thousand three

That makes two

Moments have potential
Seconds are fleeting

We can't live a life in seconds
(even though we try)

There are
You do the math
20,000 waking moments in every day

Wait, wait, what? 20,000?
No way. In a day?
Way!

Ok, ok, let that sink in

You see
We have plenty of time
To not rush
To fit in one more thing
Plenty of time
To be fully human

You see
We have plenty of time
To be fully accessible

Loving learning laughing
Leaning fully into the ordinary moments
That make up a life

Happy moments
Sad moments
Lost moments
And many, many moments of ordinary
Creating the context for
Moments of extraordinary

Historic moments
Moments of truth
Moments of inspiration

Moments of sheer boredom

Moments of fear
Moments of frustration
Moments of despair

Sometimes I just don't care
One thousand one

One thousand two
One thousand three

20,000 moments?
Then why
Why am I so overwhelmed?
Overwhelmed
With the complexity, choice, and confusion
Of this contemporary life

Take a moment
Just a moment
And breathe
One thousand one
One thousand two
One thousand three

Breathe again
More deeply this time
And pause . . .
Finding space
Between stimulus

And response

Pause . . . .
Finding space
To think
Reflect
Reframe

To be
For me
It is the safest place to be
In the moment
Not lost in an uncertain future
Not burdened by the past
Not held hostage to the numbing distractions
(of a hand-held world)

Right now
I am here
For you (me)

In the moment

One thousand one
One thousand two
One thousand three

Reflection Questions

"Where is home?"

To what degree are you still trying to fit things in—or are you truly managing the moments?

How many of your 20,000 waking moments have a special and specific purpose?

Ten

MOMENTS OF DELUSION

A question that sometimes drives me hazy: am I or are the others crazy?

— Albert Einstein

First of all, we tend to think of "being delusional" as a mental disorder. But read this definition of "delusion" from the American Psychiatric Association (APA):

A false belief based on incorrect inference about external reality that is firmly sustained despite what almost everybody else believes and despite what constitutes incontrovertible and obvious proof or evidence to the contrary. The belief is not one ordinarily accepted by other members of the person's culture or subculture. Hmmmm . . . sounds a little like leadership to me!

Here's what leaders know to be true: Sometimes we need to suspend reality while exploring some new truth. It can take us to an edge that is both exhilarating and scary. As I look back on my most important life journeys, they were always sparked by an element of delusion, a false confidence on my part (or the journey would not have begun).

Even my most recent transition from a secure corporate life at Toyota to the day-to-day entrepreneurial existence as a sole practitioner had less to do with calculated reason and more to do with a fleeting delusion that I could make a difference in the world (and not just figuratively).

Leaders, in their quest to create meaningful change, suspend the reality that pervades the lives of most to see fully what's possible. Not just what's incrementally possible, but what's "delusion-ally" possible.

No wonder the first response from our colleagues and friends is typically, Are you crazy? Well, according to the APA, yes!

The nicer term for us "delusionals" is "dreamer." However, any objective review of history will show it is the dreamers—da Vinci, Einstein, Lincoln, Earhart, etc.—who have changed our collective trajectory the most—not the realists. As we explore any of their rich biographies, we will find them hopelessly eccentric (labeled as dreamers), and not afraid to show it.

Leaders positively and judiciously use their "delusions" to change their lives and those around them for the better. Not surprisingly, several studies have shown that relationships in which both parties remained blissfully delusional about their partners (seeing both the good and the not-so-good in the most positive light) were the happiest.

So, what are your healthy delusions? Your spouse, kids, friends . . . how about your work? The world does not need one more reasonable person. It needs you—crazy you.

I know this feeling very well—even now, I have been experiencing it lately: everything seems to be ready for writing—for fulfilling my earthly duty, what's missing is the urge to believe in myself, the belief in the importance of my task, I'm lacking the energy of delusion; an earthly, spontaneous energy that's impossible to invent. And it's impossible to begin without it.

—Leo Tolstoy

DELUSIONAL YOU

Delusional you
I don't mean crazy
Like in clinical-crazy
Institutionalize-me-kind-of-crazy
Not that kind of nuthouse-crazy
You are simply

Out of touch
With what is really going on
You see
Mounting evidence suggests
You lack a healthy grounding
In an external reality
An external reality that almost everybody else believes
Except you
Delusional you

You spend little time
In the middle of your cage
Always pressing at the bars
Exploring some new truth

A truth that sets you free
Taking you to places
Both exhilarating and scary
Wow, I wish I could go there
Some time
With you

All of your journeys
Seem to have been sparked
By an element of not fully knowing
A false confidence
A rationale without reason
A hope without a hopeful foundation
But you began anyway

The world does not need
One more reasonable person
It needs you
Crazy you

I love you for that
I do

Reflection Questions
"Discovering your delusion"

Where is your genius? What is idiosyncratic and extraordinary about you?

More importantly, where is it taking you now?

EPILOGUE

The only way to keep your health is to eat what you don't want, drink what you don't like, and do what you'd rather not.

— Mark Twain

Our lives are accelerating in terms of increasing complexity, unmanageable aspects of time, escalating expectations, and declining resources. Welcome to the age of anxiety, where "busyness" captures the flow of our day.

This is not working
The center is not holding
We need to rethink our way forward

Unfortunately, our busyness also absolves us of our need to do the deeper and more profound work that will truly make a difference in our personal leadership domains.

Busyness—the wrong answer to the complexities and responsibilities of life—has never been associated with great work.

To cut through the clutter, I have been experimenting with a simple three-part process that I have memorialized onto a plastic wristband. On the band are these simple phrases:

> **Need to**
> **Want to**
> **Will do**

In a single notebook, I have created a master list of things I need to do and things I want to do. Each morning I revisit the list and I create a simple plan in my head for the three "priority" things I will do that day. Of course, I actually do dozens of things—but these will be the three things that I protect, giving me a sense of purpose for the day.

Need to do: This list is for the "responsible" me. I have my personal need-to-do's: fixing the leaky faucet (or a relationship that I let slip), refinancing the house, or transferring my retirement fund. I also have my professional need-to-do's: updating my website, preparing my taxes or making some new business contacts. There are hundreds of things that I need to do. Having a master list of them gives me a sense of control.

Want to do: This list is for the "aspirational" me. In both my personal and professional life (the lines are definitely blurring), there are things that I want to do because they give my life meaning. I want to finish my poetry book, ski ten days next year, and re-envision my consulting practice. I want to deepen some of my relationships and take my tennis game to the next level. I want to be in the best shape of my life.

Special note: I will quickly add things to my overall need-to-do and want-to-do lists (to help me feel in control so that I don't forget something) but will later cross them out if they are not truly something I want or need to do.

Will do: These are the three things (not twenty) I will commit to today. It helps me to start the day with a sense of purpose — a feeling of empowerment. Because it is only three things, it is rare that I don't get them done (especially with the darn wrist band staring at me all day). Everything else I do is a sweet bonus and doesn't feel like a burden.

My own personal rule is to every day include at least one need-to-do and one want-to-do to keep balance between my responsible and aspirational selves. The exception is vacation time, where I try to exclusively focus time on what I want to do—to fully renew the spirit. (For a free "reminder" wristband, send me a request at the e-mail address below.)

Let's keep the discussion going! Please feel free to contact me at:

mike_morrison@mac.com

Also, please check out my website to sign up for my free e-letter and lots of other free resources to help you on the journey:

www.learnplando.com

See you on the path,

Mike

A FINAL REFLECTION

You will find this quote on the column that sits in the middle of my office:

In the middle of the road of my life I awoke in the dark wood where the true way was wholly lost.

—Dante Alighieri

It has always served as an important reminder to me how being lost (and our desire to be found) defines so much of the human experience. Three points stand out in Dante's reflection:

One: We are in the middle of the road of our lives.

We are feeling the full sense of vulnerability that comes from standing alone in the middle of the road. Gone is the pre-ordained success that seemed to propel us forward, allowing us to live our lives in a future state that was "somewhere" down the road.

But for now we are "here," and with that comes the realization that until we can get comfortable with "here," our happiness and sense of peace will always be lost in a distant "there" that we never fully reach.

Two: We have awoken in the dark wood.

Could anything be more frightening than to awake in a dark and strange place? Life can feel that way today — especially in our inner, private world where darkness represents the cumulative fears, unresolved dilemmas, and the "promised" internal conversations that never happen. The darkness can even emerge in our dreams, as our subconscious gives way to an inner self-talk that is more about fear than hope, more about survival than flourishing.

However, there is also hope in this statement. To awake is to also be reborn, to be aware again — fully present to the possibilities. Awaking in the darkness reminds us that our chance for a new life will not be tied to what is familiar or comfortable.

A FINAL REFLECTION

Amazingly, the darkness begins to lose its hold on us, emboldening us to confront all that is right and wrong with our current place in the world.

Three: Where the true way was wholly lost.

In our "sleepwalking" state, we keep following the wrong god home, buying into the illusion that we could find success and security through "having"—having this stuff, having this relationship, having this degree, having this job, having these friends.

In the darkness we always get to see our true selves—a truly humbling but hopeful experience as we now see with absolute clarity that the true path is in "being," not "having."

In this time of profound change, we find ourselves ready for the renewal—and ready to face the truth about ourselves.

ABOUT THE AUTHOR

Mike Morrison is a former founder and Vice President for the University of Toyota, a corporate university he helped to launch in 1998.

Mike's passion centers on the principles and practices of developing leadership at all levels of an organization. His leadership research and hands-on experience have been documented in two popular books, *Leaning Through Meaning* (2003) and *The Other Side of the Card* (2006), and a wide range of publications including the *Harvard Business Review*. Mike has designed, developed, and managed dozens of high-impact leadership and management development programs.

Mike is also a globally recognized leader in lean thinking—with a special focus in applying "lean" principles and practices to service and knowledge environments. He has developed a wide range of education and application strategies that have produced dramatic business results.

Mike's education has taken him from the liberal arts foundations of Gonzaga University, to a University of Southern California MBA, to a doctoral degree at Claremont Graduate University's Peter F. Drucker School.

Made in the USA
Charleston, SC
02 May 2012